Jacoby's Magical Adventure

by
Querida Lu Ahn Funck

-DEDICATION-

Jacoby's Magical Adventure is dedicated
to our solider and his angels.

This is a work of fiction. Any resemblance
to actual persons, living or dead, events, or
locals is entirely coincidental.

This is Jacob Benjamin Taylor. But only his mom and dad call him that, and only when he's in trouble. Most of the time, they just call him Jacoby.

Jacoby is ten and loves to climb trees.

Jacoby lives in a big farmhouse with his parents and his dog Fluffy. He used to live in a busy city. They moved to the country when he was nine. His mom and dad said it would be quiet and peaceful.

"It's certainly quiet," Jacoby thought. "And boring."

Jacoby missed the city. The city was busy. The city was exciting! There was always something to do in the city. There were lots of kids in his old neighborhood.

In the country, he was alone. And lonely.

One day when Jacoby was bored, his mother sent him to explore the attic. The attic was full of things that had been left behind by the previous owners. In the bottom of an old trunk, he found a wooden box. Jacoby brushed dust off the box and saw two words carved into the lid. Magic Memories. He shook the box and flipped it over. There was a small key taped to the bottom. Jacoby whooped with excitement and ran down the stairs to find Fluffy.

"Look what I found, Fluffy!"

They looked at the box together. Jacoby shook it gently for Fluffy to listen to. Fluffy sniffed at the box and gave it a small lick.

"What do you think is inside?" Jacoby asked. "I don't know either Fluffy," he answered. "Shall we guess?"

They guessed for a few minutes, then Jacoby put the key in the lock and turned it until it clicked.

The box was full of tiny treasures.

A lock of hair....
A deck of cards....
Some old coins....

A fat blue pencil and a stack of tiny drawings....

Jacoby liked the drawings. There was one of a cabin. And one of a bench on the bank of a river. And one of an old stone gate. Like the ones he saw in his history book.

The drawings showed beautiful places that Jacoby would like to visit some day.

The sunlight bounced off the coins in the box. Jacoby noticed a piece of paper taped to the inside of the lid.

Something was written on the paper.

It was a poem.

"Hold in your heart... What you desire. Draw what you need... to remember and inspire."

"Do you think these are places someone visited, Fluffy? I bet they drew them to remember them."

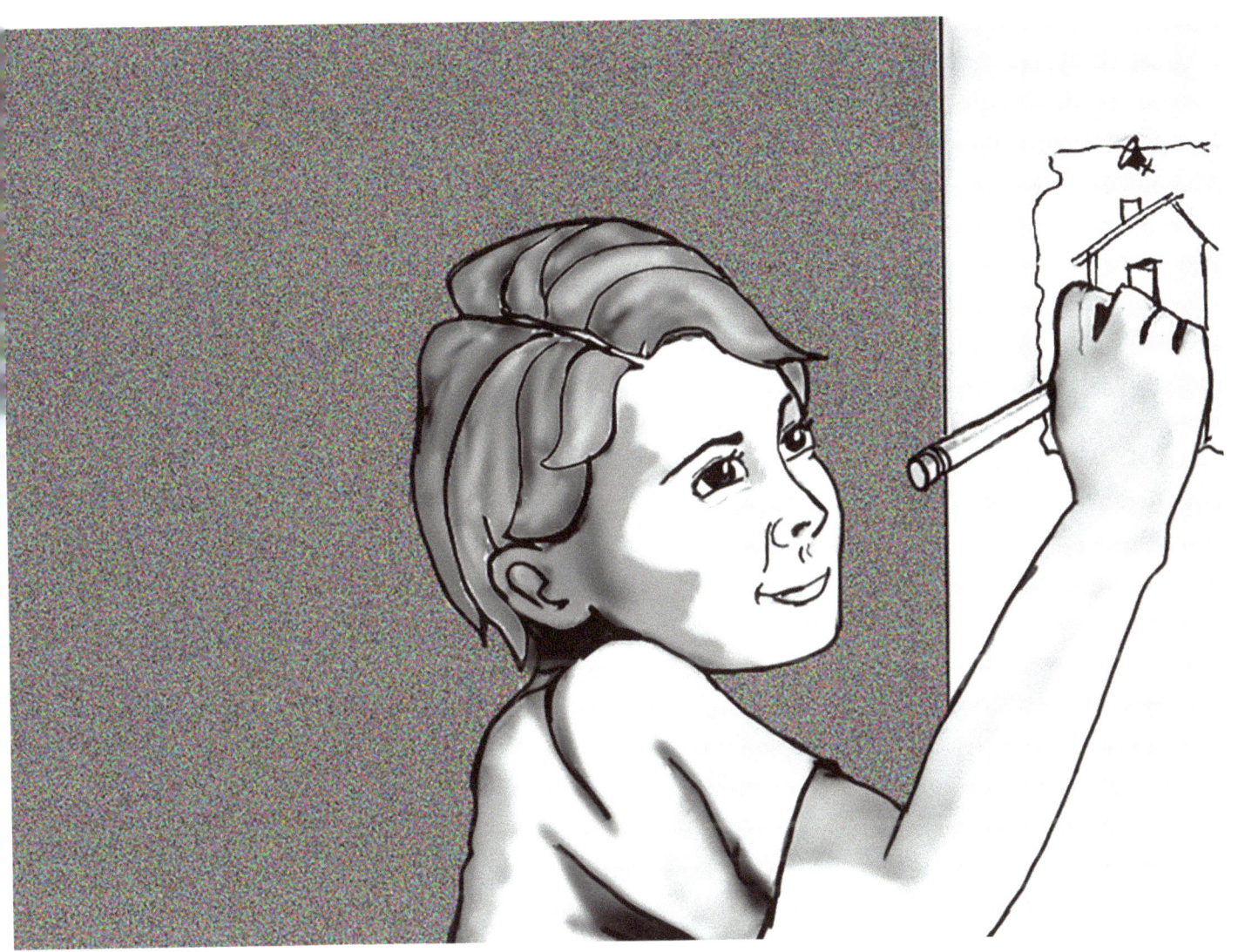

Jacoby grabbed some paper from his desk and picked up the fat blue pencil from the box. He tacked the paper to his wall and drew what he wanted to visit, what he missed the most. He tucked the extra paper and the pencil in his back pocket while he looked at his drawing.

"Hold in your heart... What you desire. Draw what you need... to remember and inspire."

Jacoby felt dizzy and the room began to spin.

When the spinning stopped, he was standing in front of his **old** house in the old neighborhood!

Two girls, one blonde and one brunette, sat on the steps of his old porch and stared at him in surprise.

"Who are you?" Jacoby and the blonde girl asked at the same time.

That made the other girl giggle.

"My name is Jacoby. I used to live here."

"I live here now. I'm Aislynn." Aislynn said.

The other girl tugged on Aislynn's sleeve. "This is Keir. She's my sister."

I wish you still lived here," Aislynn pouted, "There's nothing fun to do."

"Why would you say that? This is a fun neighborhood!"

"Have you met the Olson boys yet? They ride their bikes up and down the block. I bet they'd let you ride with them," Jacoby suggested.

"Kimi and Joe live at the other end of the block in the blue house. They like to build things."

"There are some older kids in the neighborhood too. Jackie, Martha and Joanne are always jumping rope."

"And Jackie's brother Kyle is really good at teaching the younger kids to Double Dutch. Can you Double Dutch?"

The girls were excited now.

Jacoby ran up to the door of his old house and knocked. The girls' dad answered.

"Hi, sir. I'm Jacoby," he introduced himself.

"I used to live here. I'm back visiting and met Aislynn and Keir. Would it be okay if I showed them around the neighborhood?"

The girls and their dad were delighted and agreed.

First, he took them to the school play-ground.

They met the Tyler triplets and played T-Ball.

Keir was a natural. She hit a home run and got to run all the bases and slide into home plate!

Then Jacoby took them to the park where they met Parker and Megan.

The park was full of butterflies!

Megan let Aislynn borrow her bug net.

Jacoby cheered Aislynn on as she chased the butterflies.

Keir saw some kids playing in the sand pit and went to join them.

Keir built sandcastles with
a group of toddlers.

Later, Jacoby took the girls to the library.

They were just in time for story hour. They joined a group of kids to listen to the librarian read fairytales.

Aislynn and Timmy looked through a picture book.

Keir and Tyrone looked at book about Clydesdale horses.

Jacoby helped the girls get their own library cards. They picked out a tall stack of books to take home.

The girls were excited to tell their dad about their adventure and show him all the books they brought home to read!

The girls thanked Jacoby for showing them around the neighborhood.

He hugged them and said, "You don't have to be lonely. You just needed to go exploring and meet some new friends."

Jacoby waved goodbye and promised to come visit them again soon.

He took the fat blue pencil out of his pocket and drew a picture of Fluffy. Then he closed his eyes and recited the poem.

"Hold in your heart... What you desire. Draw what you need..."

He felt the familiar spin of magic. When he opened his eyes, he was back in his room with Fluffy.

Jacoby picked up the box and found the drawing of the stone gate. He tacked it to his wall and looked down at Fluffy, taking a firm hold of her collar.

"Are you ready for an adventure, Fluffy? We don't have to be lonely either. We just need to go exploring." Jacoby looked at the drawing of the stone gate again and recited the poem.

Jacoby's adventures are
just beginning!

I hope you enjoyed your time with
Jacoby and Fluffy.

Please consider leaving a review on
Amazon or Goodreads
and share this book with a friend!

Bonus materials are available on
www.dreamtimeillustrations.com.

Be sure to check it out!

www.ingramcontent.com/pod-product-compliance
Lightning Source LLC
Chambersburg PA
CBHW041526120626

46551CB00018B/2581